FIRST 15 LESSONS

DRUMS

by Alan Arber

Includes Audio & Video Access

T0071511

ISBN 978-1-5400-0294-5

HAL•LEONARD®

7777 W. BLUEMOUND RD. P.O. BOX 13819 MILWAUKEE, WI 53213

Copyright © 2018 by HAL LEONARD LLC
International Copyright Secured   All Rights Reserved

For all works contained herein:
Unauthorized copying, arranging, adapting, recording, Internet posting,
public performance, or other distribution of the printed or recorded music
in this publication is an infringement of copyright.
Infringers are liable under the law.

Visit Hal Leonard Online at
www.halleonard.com

PLAYBACK+
Speed • Pitch • Balance • Loop

To access audio, video, and extra content visit:
www.halleonard.com/mylibrary

Enter Code
2908-7636-0683-6035

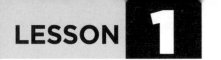
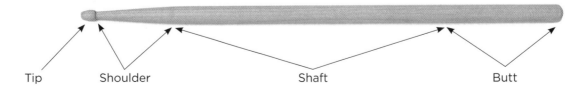 Your first lesson involves learning the parts of the drumset that you will be using, as well as getting yourself properly positioned with sticks in hand, ready to play your first song.

PARTS OF THE DRUMSET

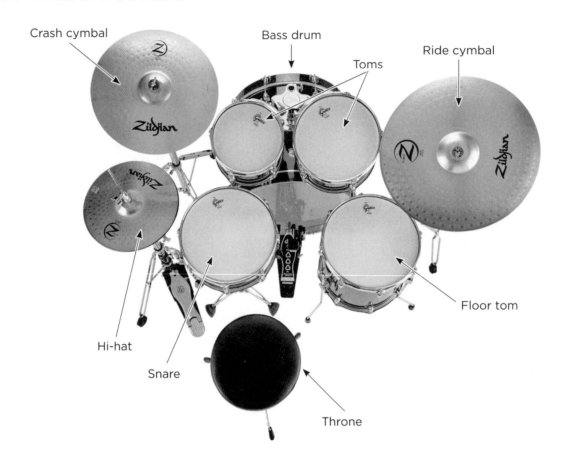

Crash cymbal · Bass drum · Toms · Ride cymbal · Hi-hat · Snare · Throne · Floor tom

SITTING AT THE DRUMSET

Sit down at the drumset and adjust the seat (also called the *drum throne*) up or down or by moving the seat back or forth. While your legs are bent at a 90-degree angle, rest your right foot on the bass drum pedal and your left foot on the hi-hat pedal. Press your left foot down until the two hi-hat cymbals are closed.

Here is an overhead photo showing how to sit at the drumset. The snare drum is between the legs and the hi-hat cymbals are just far enough to the left so they don't overlap the top of your snare drum. To achieve the 90-degree angle with your legs, adjust yourself or your seat. Your legs should not be touching the snare drum at all.

HOLDING YOUR STICKS

Tip · Shoulder · Shaft · Butt

Pick up your drumstick with your right hand and loosely wrap all of your fingers around it. Put the pad of your thumb on the stick and adjust your hand so that there is roughly two inches of the stick exposed below your pinky finger. Use the adjacent photo to help with proper finger position. Follow the same instructions for holding the stick in your left hand. This grip is called *matched grip*.

PLAYING THE HI-HAT

While sitting at your drumset with your sticks in hand, lift your right arm and touch the tip of your stick to the hi-hat cymbal. Do **not** lift your elbow! It should be directly under your shoulder and completely relaxed on the side of your body. While touching your stick to the cymbal, picture an imaginary straight line from your elbow all the way to the tip of the stick.

You are now ready to play the hi-hat. Every note you play is going to be a tap with the tip or shoulder of the stick and a lift. Don't press down on the cymbal with your stick after you hit it. As soon as you hit the cymbal, lift the stick from it by bending your wrist.

The most common rhythm that is played on the hi-hat is the eighth note. The following are eighth notes in groups of 2 and in groups of 4.

Throughout this method, there are going to be four beats in every *measure* (also called *bars*). The eight eighth notes above equal four beats. Count the eighth notes while playing them: "1-and, 2-and, 3-and, 4-and" (the "ands" are typically notated with a "+" or "&" sign), then repeat. Every time you repeat back to count 1, a new measure begins.

Bar lines are used to separate measures. Play the pattern below on the hi-hat. Eighth notes played on the hi-hat are notated on the top of the musical staff, written as Xs and with the stem pointing upward. (**Note:** "R" stands for right hand and "L" for left hand.)

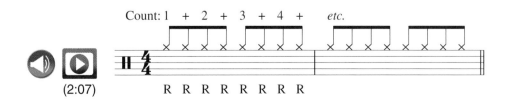

(2:07)

THE BASS DRUM

The bass drum is the biggest drum of the kit and has a foot pedal attached. While sitting at the drumset, your right foot should be resting on the bass drum pedal. Play the bass drum by pushing down on the pedal, either with your heel up or your heel down (flat-footed) on the pedal. It is up to you, but never let your toes leave the pedal when you lift your foot up.

A quarter note is equivalent to one beat, and there are four beats in each measure (counted: 1, 2, 3, 4). A quarter note on the bass drum is notated on the bottom space of the musical staff, with the stem pointing up or down.

You'll also see the time signature at the front of the exercises. The *time signature* tells you how many beats are in a measure (top number) and which beat value receives one count (bottom number).

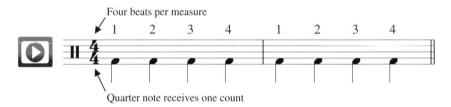

Let's play the bass drum and hi-hat together. The following exercise shows the hi-hat playing eighth notes and the bass drum playing quarter notes:

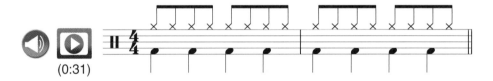

(0:31)

THE SNARE DRUM

Sitting at your drumset, the snare drum is the drum between your legs. It is played with your left hand. Try hitting the center of the snare drum with the tip of the stick. Don't press the stick down on the drumhead; instead, tap the drum and lift the stick from the head (similar to how the hi-hat is played with the other hand). Adjust the height of the snare drum so that you can hit the drumhead comfortably without contacting the rim of the drum or your leg.

The snare drum is written on the second space from the top of the musical staff, with the stem facing either up or down.

GROOVE #1

It's time to put all of the instruments (snare, hi-hat, and bass drum) together and start playing your first groove. First, there is some musical notation you need to know.

Repeats

A *repeat sign* tells you to repeat the previous measure or tells you how many times to repeat the previous measure:

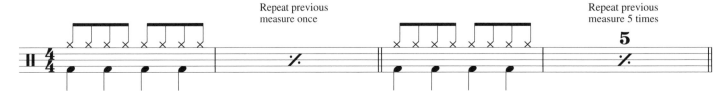

This type of repeat sign tells you to repeat the previous number of measures indicated (in this case, the previous two measures are repeated):

The symbols shown here indicate you should repeat everything in between them. Sometimes this will take you back to the start of the music. Only repeat what is between these two signs:

A *first ending* and a *second ending* can be used if you are repeating a section but jumping to an alternate ending. Here's how that works: in the example below, play the first three measures and then repeat back to the beginning; next, play the first two measures again before jumping over the first ending to the second ending (skipping the third measure the second time through and playing the fourth measure).

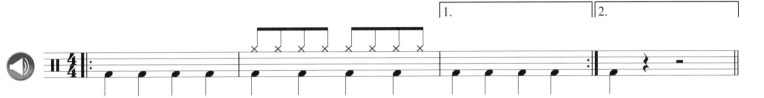

Rests

Rests are intervals of silence when the instrument doesn't play (but are still counted).

Whole Rest = four beats of silence:

Quarter Rest = one full beat of silence:

Two measures of rest:

Half Rest = two beats of silence:

Four measures of rest:

"Another One Bites the Dust"

(1:34)

Words and Music by John Deacon
Copyright © 1980 Queen Music Ltd.
All Rights Administered by Sony/ATV Music Publishing LLC, 424 Church Street, Suite 1200, Nashville, TN 37219
International Copyright Secured   All Rights Reserved

Additional Listening

"Uptown Funk" Mark Ronson/Bruno Mars

"Brown Sugar" The Rolling Stones

"Another Brick in the Wall, Pt. 2" Pink Floyd

"Old Time Rock & Roll" Bob Seger & the Silver Bullet Band

"Moves Like Jagger" Maroon 5

"Shut Up and Dance" Walk the Moon

"I Gotta Feeling" The Black Eyed Peas

GROOVE #2

While Groove #1 had the bass drum playing on all four beats (1, 2, 3, and 4), Groove #2 has the bass drum playing only beats 1 and 3. This may take a little getting used to, but you should learn to play both of these grooves quite well because they are arguably the most used drum beats ever played.

"Every Breath You Take"

This song starts with a *flam* (see below) on the snare drum as a pickup note on beat 4 before the groove enters. A *pickup note* (or notes) precede the first full measure of a song.

(1:29)

Music and Lyrics by Sting
Copyright © 1983 G.M. Sumner
All Rights Administered by Sony/ATV Music Publishing LLC, 424 Church Street, Suite 1200, Nashville, TN 37219
International Copyright Secured   All Rights Reserved

Flam

A *flam* is a drum stroke that consists of two notes: the primary note and the grace note. The primary note is the louder note and the grace note is the quieter one, played slightly before the primary note. The two notes take up one full beat. Be sure to practice alternating hands. You can practice flams anywhere, even without drumsticks. It's a movement your hands need to get used to.

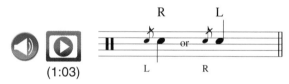

(1:03)

Additional Listening

"Billie Jean" Michael Jackson

"Hella Good" No Doubt

"Kashmir" Led Zeppelin

"Best of My Love" Eagles

"Peter Gunn" Henry Mancini

"The Stroke" Billy Squier

"Back in Black" AC/DC

"Dreams" Fleetwood Mac

"Stayin' Alive" Bee Gees

GROOVE #3

Groove #3 has two extra bass drum notes added to the beat. Notice that the bass drum now plays two eighth notes on beats 1 and 3 instead of just one quarter note. Note that the hi-hat is playing simultaneously with all of the bass drum notes. Play this groove while counting eighth notes as before.

Example 1

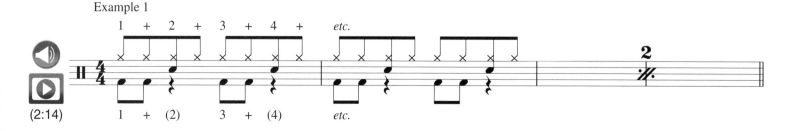

(2:14)

MOVING THE BASS DRUM AROUND

Let's try putting the bass drum on different counts. The following example shows the bass drum playing on beat 1 and the "and," or *upbeat*, of beat 2. The silence on the bass drum on beat 2 is notated by an *eighth rest*, which lasts a half beat (just like the eighth note), followed by a single eighth note on the "and" of beat 2.

Example 2

(2:37)

COUNTING MEASURES

In many cases, the drums don't play immediately when the song starts. The way to figure out exactly when the drums enter is by counting measures. The first measure is counted normally (1, 2, 3, 4), while every measure afterwards is counted by replacing beat 1 with the number of the measure you are on: "**1** 2 3 4, **2** 2 3 4, **3** 2 3 4, **4** 2 3 4," etc. This Tom Petty song has a four-bar guitar introduction before the groove.

"Free Fallin'"

Words and Music by Tom Petty and Jeff Lynne
Copyright © 1989 Gone Gator Music and EMI April Music Inc.
All Rights for EMI April Music Inc. Administered by Sony/ATV Music Publishing LLC, 424 Church Street, Suite 1200, Nashville, TN 37219
All Rights Reserved   Used by Permission

If we move the bass drum over to the "and" of beat 3, we get a whole new groove.

Example 3

(2:59)

Finally, putting an eighth rest on beat 1 gives the groove quite a different sound.

Additional Listening

"We Will Rock You" Queen (Example 1)

"Sweet Home Alabama" Lynyrd Skynyrd (Example 2)

"Heathens" Twenty One Pilots (Example 3)

"Sugar" Maroon 5 (Example 2)

"Give Me One Reason" Tracy Chapman (Example 2)

"Kiss" Prince (Example 2)

"You Shook Me All Night Long" AC/DC (Example 3)

"Centerfold" The J. Geils Band (Example 3)

FILLS

A *drum fill* is a break in the groove or a short passage used to "fill" in between sections of a song. Drum fills are used to let the listener know that there is a change coming in the song. It helps build excitement and is an interesting way to signal the end of a four- or eight-bar phrase.

Drum fills can vary in length and sound, depending on which drums you use. Fills can be played on one drum or a number of drums. You can use the tom-toms to make it more exciting and interesting.

EIGHTH-NOTE FILLS

The first few examples include eighth-note fills starting on the third beat of the fourth measure, so there will be a total of four notes played in each fill. These are called four-measure phrases. *Phrases* help separate different musical ideas. Imagine that the four measures are a sentence, and the fill ends the sentence with a cymbal crash as punctuation. A cymbal crash is notated with an "X" on the first ledger line above the staff. *Ledger lines* are short lines written above or below the staff.

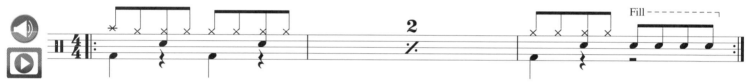

Now let's use the three tom-toms to play the same fill. The high tom is notated on the top space of the staff, the low tom on the second line just below that, and the floor tom on the second space from the bottom.

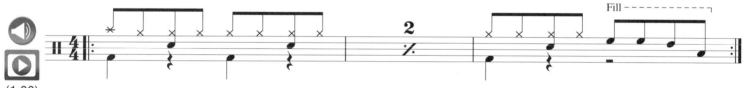

(1:00)

This next fill is used in the chorus of ZZ Top's "Sharp Dressed Man." It is important to note that the crash cymbal at the end of the fill marks the beginning (beat 1) of the next four-measure phrase.

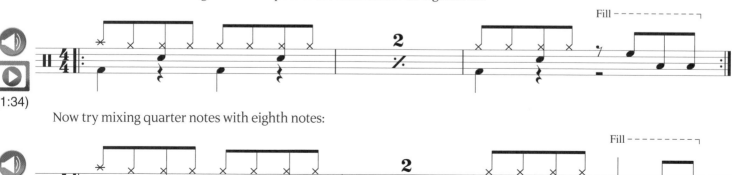

Words and Music by Billy F Gibbons, Dusty Hill and Frank Lee Beard
Copyright © 1983 Music Of Stage Three
All Rights Administered by Stage Three Music (US) Inc., a BMG Chrysalis company
All Rights Reserved   Used by Permission

You can also remove an eighth note so part of the fill includes an eighth rest:

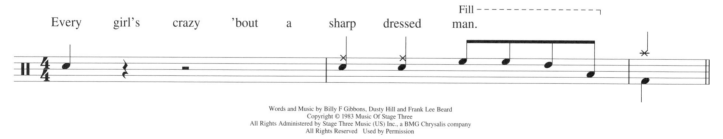

(1:34)

Now try mixing quarter notes with eighth notes:

(2:05)

MORE EIGHTH-NOTE FILLS

You can also combine the foot with the hands to come up with some interesting variations. The following fills are preceded by three measures of groove, with the fill starting on beat 3 of the fourth measure.

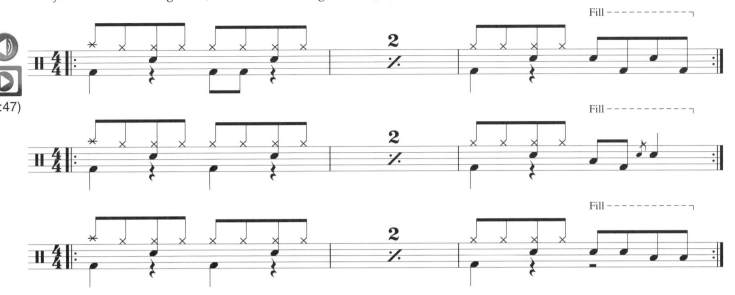

(2:47)

You can create a very powerful fill by playing eighth-note flams with the right hand on the floor tom and the left hand on the snare drum. Remember: when playing a flam, although you're playing two notes, it should take up the rhythmic space of only one note.

(4:28)

The next fill starts on beat 1 of the fourth measure and lasts the entire measure. There are now eight notes in your fill.

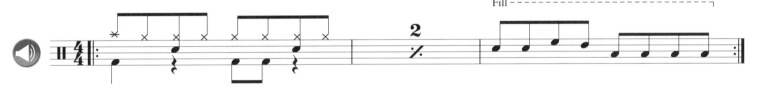

DOTTED QUARTER NOTES

You are going to start seeing notes that are accompanied by a dot. A *dot* increases the duration of the note that precedes it by half of that note's value. For example, when you see a dotted quarter note, it is equivalent to one-and-a-half beats. The dot adds a half beat to the quarter note. The extra duration is not played; it is just **counted**.

Play the dotted note on the beat it lands on and count the extra duration. Then simply add an eighth note to finish the rest of the beat.

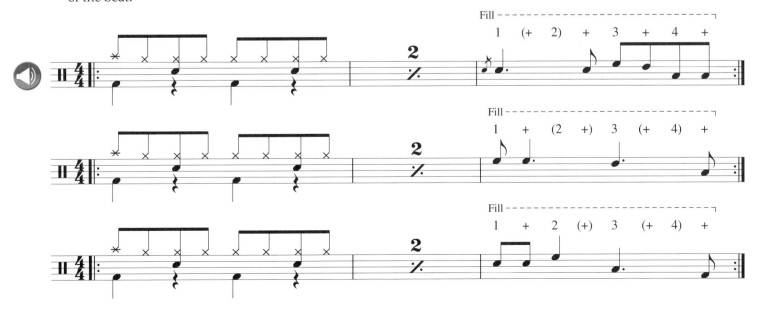

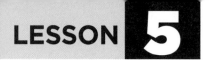

16TH NOTES

16th notes look like this:

A 16th rest looks like this:

Two or more 16th notes are connected by a double beam and are counted like this: "1-e-and-a, 2-e-and-a, 3-e-and-a, 4-e-and-a," etc. Notice that the numbers and the "ands" are still present, with the other 16th notes simply filling the spaces in between. The relationships between quarter, eighth, and 16th notes and rests are shown in the downloadable rhythm charts. Notice how everything lines up. Try counting one rhythm out loud while simultaneously playing another rhythm on a drum or practice pad. For example, play eighth notes while counting 16th notes. A 16th rest has the same rhythmic value as a 16th note but is silent.

> A PDF containing several helpful rhythm charts is available for download with this book!
> Simply visit **www.halleonard.com/mylibrary** and enter the code found on page 1 to access it.

To get used to changing between quarter notes, eighth notes, and 16th notes, play through the following three exercises without stopping. Play the pedal of the hi-hat with your left foot on the quarter notes. The hi-hat pedal is notated with an X in the space directly below the staff, with the stem facing down.

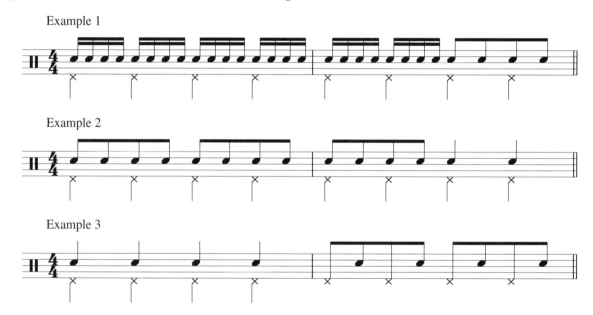

16TH-NOTE FILLS

Now try a drum groove with different 16th-note fills at the end of each four-bar phrase. The following fills are going to start on beat 1 of the fourth measure.

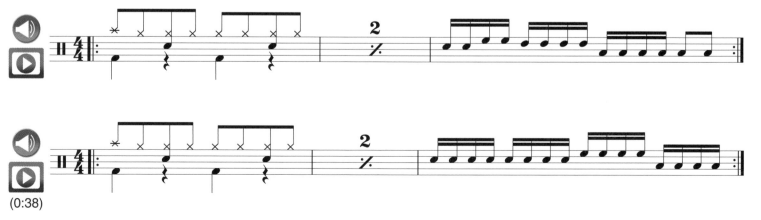

(0:38)

The following fills still start on beat 1 of the fourth measure, but we have eliminated the last 16th note of each beat. You will see in the notation that there is no 16th rest included because the eighth note that falls on the "and" is equal to two 16th notes (or 16th rests), so there's no need to include the 16th rest. The count of the beat that is missing is in parentheses, but still needs to be counted.

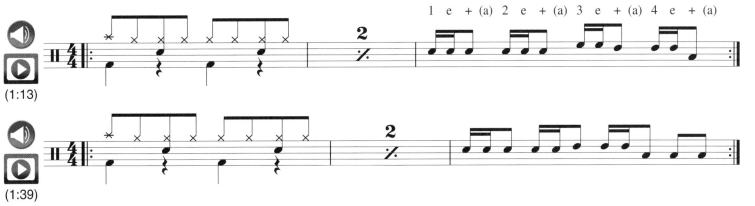

We can also take out the 16th note that falls on beat 3 or beat 4—or both.

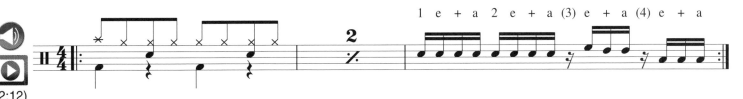

Below is a popular fill in which the 16th note that falls on the "e" count is eliminated. Again, there is no need to include a 16th rest because of the eighth note that precedes it.

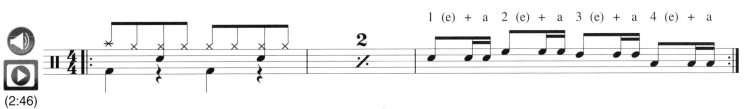

Finally, let's remove the 16th notes on the "+" (or "and") count of the fill:

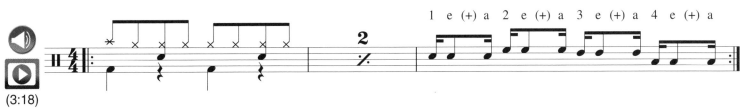

DOTTED EIGHTH-NOTE/16TH-NOTE GROUPING

Playing a dotted eighth note connected to a 16th note is equivalent to the duration of four 16th notes:

Play the first note (which is count 1), count "e and," and then finish the beat with a single 16th note. The following fills include dotted eighth-note/16th-note groupings. See the previous downloadable rhythm charts for an additional chart that shows the relationship between regular notes and dotted notes.

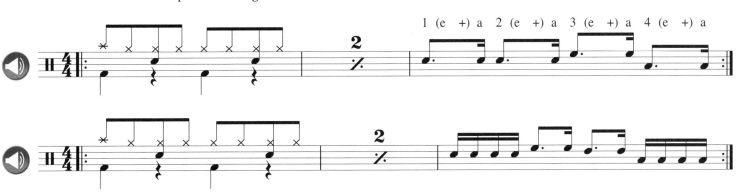

11

HAND/FOOT GROOVE COMBINATIONS

In the following examples, we will mix up 16th notes between the snare and bass drum and look at different popular songs that use these ideas. This form of playing is called *syncopation*, whereby *accents* (notes or rhythms that are emphasized) are placed where they wouldn't normally occur.

The first example has the snare playing on the "a" of beat 2 and the "e" of beat 3. Remember: the counts inside the parentheses are to be counted but not played; they are included for reference only.

2 (e +) a

This next example is a very popular drum groove. The bass drum 16th note falls on the "a" of beat 1. Note that the single 16th notes in these examples are played alone; they fall **between** the hi-hat notes. Do **not** speed up your hi-hat playing; instead, continue playing steady eighth notes.

(0:52)

1 (e +) a

The example below has two bass drum notes a 16th note apart. This is called a *double stroke* on the bass drum and can be challenging, but it's imperative that every drummer learns it. After playing the "a" on beat 2, you need to immediately kick again on beat 3:

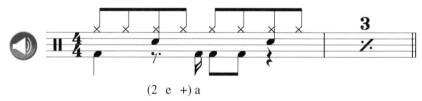

(2 e +) a

The following groove has the snare drum playing on the "a" of beat 2:

(1:16)

> **Additional Listening**
>
> "Loser" Beck
> "Give It Away" Red Hot Chili Peppers
> "Crazy" Seal
>
> "Walk This Way" Aerosmith
> "Hard to Handle" The Black Crowes

HAND/FOOT FILL COMBINATIONS

The following fill ideas show how you can play 16th notes between the hands and the bass drum (start all fills with your right hand). These fill examples are meant to start on beat 1 of the fourth measure after playing three measures of a groove of your choice. Only the fills are played on the accompanying audio tracks.

(1:47)

(2:03)

CHART READING

The following notation is popular if the musician is reading a chart. A *chart* can be described as a "blueprint" of a song. It shows you exactly how to play a song, even if you've never heard it before. If you're given a drum chart, the drum groove won't be written out in many cases. Instead, the following diagonal lines in the measures simply mean to play the groove in the style written at the top of the music.

Another way a chart can indicate how many measures a groove is played is with a number at the top:

In many cases, the music that is written on a chart is either "cues" or specific fills that the arranger wants you to play. Otherwise, the word "fill" is written in that measure and it's up to you to decide what to play. Here are more chart samples you might encounter:

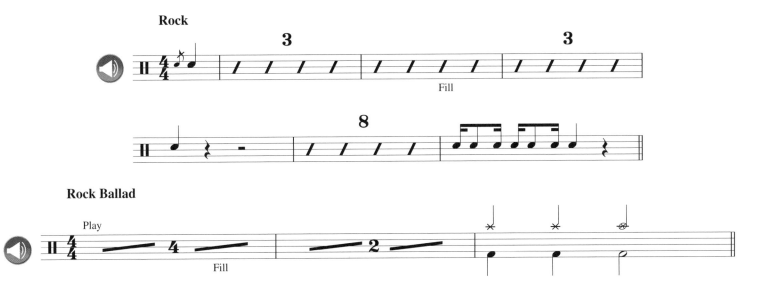

NAVIGATION SIGNS

D.S., or *Dal Segno*, tells you to repeat back to an earlier section of the song, which is marked by the following sign: 𝄋

D.S. al Coda means, after returning to the sign, play from the sign to a "To Coda" marking, then jump to the Coda section at the end of the music.

D.C. al Coda is a term telling you to repeat back to the beginning of the music and play until the Coda symbol, then jump to the Coda section at the end.

Fine is a musical term that marks the end of the song, usually following a D.C. or D.S. marking.

Coda is the concluding section of a song that contains additional measures to the basic song structure.

LESSON 7

Demo   Play-Along

"SMELLS LIKE TEEN SPIRIT"

Here is a full song to study and play. Notice the tempo marking at the top of the tune. This gives you the *BPM*, or beats per minute, of the song. Plug this into your metronome when you practice, but first start at a slower speed and work your way up to it.

A free online metronome comes with this book! Simply visit **www.halleonard.com/mylibrary** and enter the code found on page 1 to access it.

Words and Music by Kurt Cobain, Krist Novoselic and Dave Grohl
Copyright © 1991 The End Of Music, Primary Wave Tunes, M.J. Twelve Music and Murky Slough Music
All Rights for The End Of Music and Primary Wave Tunes Administered by BMG Rights Management (US) LLC
All Rights Reserved   Used by Permission

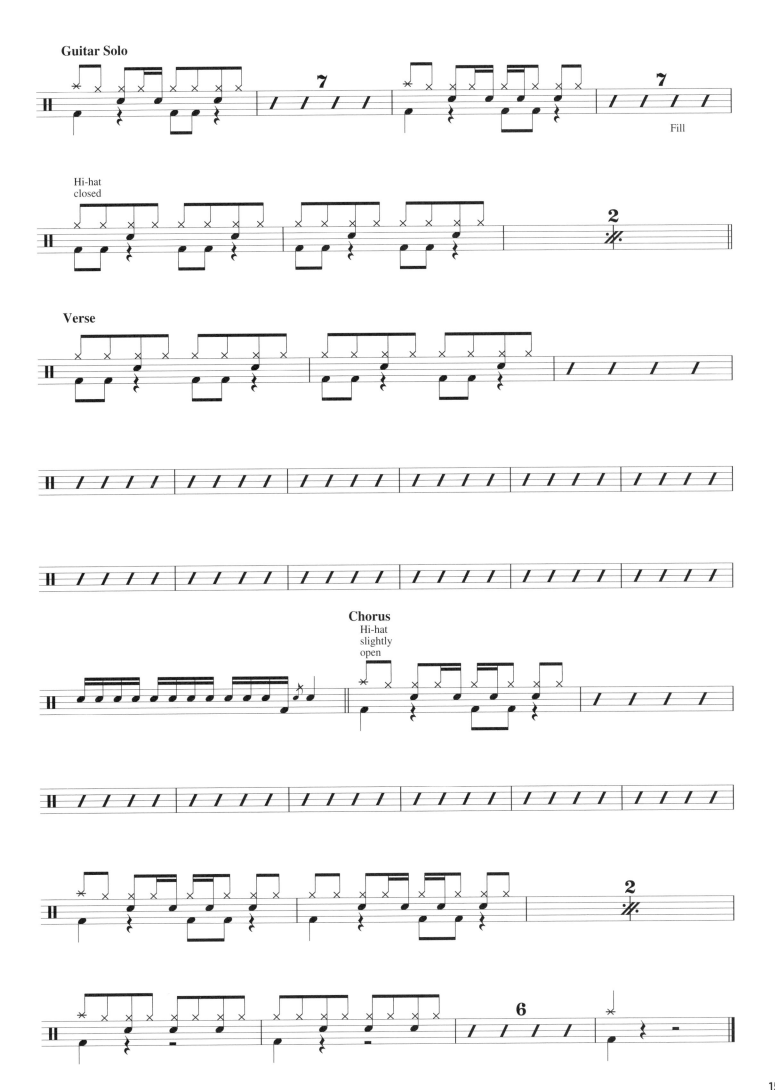

RUDIMENTS

We have been covering different grooves on the drum kit and experimenting with moving the bass drum or snare drum around to different parts of the beat. This lesson is going to cover some fundamentals to help your playing advance to the next level. The following examples are called *drum rudiments*. A drum rudiment is essentially a sticking pattern. All of the sticking patterns you have been playing on the drum kit come from specific drum rudiments. We will be covering some important rudiments that are practical and used consistently on the drum kit.

THE ROLL

(0:36)

A *roll* on the snare drum consists of hitting the drum and lightly pressing the stick down on the drumhead to produce a buzz or multiple bounces. If you press down too hard, the buzz will be too short, and if there isn't enough pressure, the bounce of the stick will be too open-sounding.

Start the roll by lightly pressing the stick on the drumhead with the right hand and then the left hand. While switching back and forth from hand to hand, make sure the buzzes are overlapping and not creating any space. The extra bounces should be produced by the natural stick rebound and **not** extra strokes made by the hand. In music notation, a roll is notated with lines above or below the note.

The examples below are different types of roll rudiments, using half notes and whole notes, along with other rhythms previously learned. Use a metronome for each example, moving from slow to fast tempos.

The Single Stroke Roll
This is played by alternating right and left hands, at a consistent, fast speed.

*A little faster on each repeat.

The Double-Stroke Roll (or Long Roll)

(1:07)

This is played with a stroke and a bounce in each hand. Each stroke produces two notes. Also in this example, notice the notes connected by a curved line. This is called a *tie* and indicates that the two notes are to be played as a single note, with the duration equaling the sum of the two notes.

The Five-Stroke Roll
This is based off the double-stroke roll and consists of two double strokes and a single, resulting in five total strokes.

(1:34)

The Six-Stroke Roll
This has mixed single and double strokes.

The Seven-Stroke Roll

This consists of three double strokes and one single.

(2:05)

The Nine-Stroke Roll

This consists of four double strokes and one single.

FLAM

The flam is a rudiment and was introduced earlier in this book. Now you'll learn how to alternate between right- and left-handed flams and when to use them, because you will be using both on the drumset.

Swiss Triplet

(**Note:** you'll learn more about the triplet rhythm later. For now, practice the sticking pattern of this rudiment.)

Flam Tap

Flam Accent

PARADIDDLE

The *paradiddle* rudiment combines single and double strokes and has a number of variations, which every drummer should know how to play. Paradiddles help movement around the drumset become smoother and faster. Remember to bounce the stick whenever you see a double stroke, and try to make all of the notes evenly spaced.

(2:27)

Single Paradiddle

Single Paradiddle-Diddle

Double Paradiddle

Inverted Paradiddle

Paradiddles also produce great groove ideas. The challenge to playing these correctly is to accent beats 2 and 4. For these examples, the snare and bass drum are beamed together and downstemmed so you can see the paradiddle patterns.

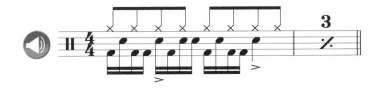

16TH-NOTE GROOVES

The following lesson teaches how to play 16th notes on the hi-hat with either one or two hands, depending on the song's tempo.

In order to play this groove, the two hands play 16th notes on the hi-hat, except for beats 2 and 4. On those two beats, the right hand plays the snare drum while the left hand stays on the hi-hat.

The bass drum follows the same rules as in past lessons. For now, practice with the bass drum on beats 1 and 3.

(0:32)

VARIATIONS

In the next example, the bass drum plays on beats 1, 2, 3, and 4.

(0:51)

Here are a few other bass drum patterns:

(1:06)

"Rock with You"

This song has a bass drum double stroke on the "a" of beat 2 and on beat 3.

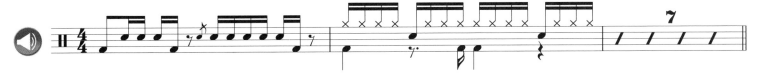

Additional Listening

"Smoke on the Water" Deep Purple

"Turn Me Loose" Loverboy

"Crazy Train" Ozzy Osbourne

"Everlong" Foo Fighters

"The Way It Is" Bruce Hornsby

THE MOELLER METHOD

(1:22)

The *Moeller Method* is a technique used by drummers to develop more control, power, and speed. This is essential to master the following grooves, which involve one hand playing 16th notes on the hi-hat. The following explanation will be focusing on the right hand, but mastering this technique with both hands is strongly recommended.

This method relies on a "whipping" motion, in which the shoulder of the drumstick strikes the hi-hat on beat 1, immediately followed by a pulling-up motion on the back of the stick, causing the tip to hit again on "e." The same sequence of motion repeats for "and" and "a," respectively. This results in accents on the eighth notes that occur within the 16th-note pattern. Keep the bass drum on beats 1 and 3 and the snare drum on beats 2 and 4.

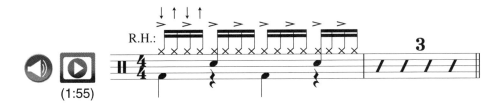

(1:55)

You can see the accents on the eighth notes, and the non-accented notes on the "e" and "a." It's extremely important to approach this technique knowing that you need to achieve two sounds with one stroke: the whip down and the lift up.

Additional Listening

"Use Me" Bill Withers

"I Keep Forgettin'" Michael McDonald

"You Look Good" Lady Antebellum

"Tom Sawyer" Rush

"Hold the Line" Toto

CUT TIME

This lesson will be covering a concept called *cut time*, or *alla breve*. Cut time is an alternate way to count 4/4 time at faster tempos. It makes counting and conducting more convenient, resulting in music that flows better.

The time signature for cut time is 2/2. There are two beats in each measure and the half note receives one beat. When a piece of music is in cut time, the musician typically will see the cut-time symbol rather than the 2/2 time signature:

In cut time, the music looks the same but is counted differently. That's because every note is cut in half:

$\mathbf{o}$ = 2 beats   = 1/2 beat

= 1 beat   = 1/4 beat

These two examples show how to count 4/4 rhythms in cut time:

GROOVES IN CUT TIME

Play the following groove while counting it in cut time. Remember: there is no need to count in cut time unless the song is too fast and counting in 4/4 becomes difficult.

The eighth notes on the hi-hat will be too fast to play, so you play quarter notes on the hi-hat in cut time, which are now counted as eighth notes.

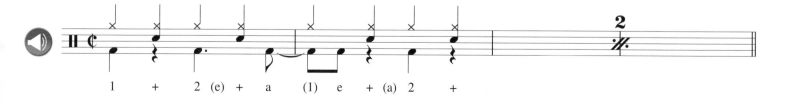

"Bang Bang"

This is a very fast example of counting in cut time:

Words and Music by Billie Joe Armstrong, Mike Dirnt and Tre Cool
© 2016 W.B.M. MUSIC CORP. and GREEN DAZE MUSIC
All Rights Administered by W.B.M. MUSIC CORP.
All Rights Reserved   Used by Permission

TRAIN BEAT

The train beat can be counted in 4/4 or cut time, depending on its tempo. The beat emulates the sound of a train driving by, hence the name. Pay close attention to the accents on the snare drum—they are key to making this beat sound good. Here is the train beat written both ways:

Additional Listening

"Folsom Prison Blues" Johnny Cash

"Liza Jane" Vince Gill

"American Idiot" Green Day

"Stickshifts and Safetybelts" Cake

"Ballroom Blitz" Sweet

"The Devil Went Down to Georgia" The Charlie Daniels Band

"Face the Face" Pete Townshend

"Two Step" Dave Matthews Band

"New Way Home" Foo Fighters

"Let's Go Crazy" Prince

"American Girl" Tom Petty

ODD TIME SIGNATURES

We've covered time signatures, or *meters*, in past lessons, so you already know the top number tells you how many beats are in each measure. So far, we've been playing musical examples and songs written in 4/4 time (and cut time). In this lesson, however, we will be covering songs written in odd time signatures, in which the top number is 3, 5, 7, or even higher.

Our first time signature is 3/4. The top number tells us there are three beats in each measure and the bottom number tells us that the quarter note receives one beat. Play the following example to help you get used to this new time signature:

You will often see time signatures changing right in the middle of a song or a piece of music. Try playing the following short solo, which features changing meters. Sit at the drumset and play quarter notes on the hi-hat pedal with your left foot throughout the piece.

ODD TIME SIGNATURES IN POPULAR MUSIC

There are thousands of songs with time signatures other than 4/4. Challenge yourself to play some of the most popular ones.

You'll notice the time signature's bottom number changes on some of these examples. When the bottom number is 8, the eighth note receives one full beat. The 16th note gets a half beat and is counted "1 + 2 + 3 + 4 +," etc.

"Solsbury Hill"

This is one of the most popular odd-meter songs ever recorded. The song is in 7/4 and the guitar plays pickup notes before the drums enter.

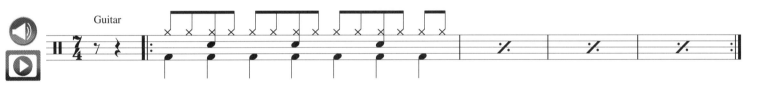

Words and Music by Peter Gabriel
Copyright © 1979 Real World Music Ltd.
All Rights Administered by Sony/ATV Music Publishing LLC, 424 Church Street, Suite 1200, Nashville, TN 37219
International Copyright Secured   All Rights Reserved

"(You Make Me Feel Like) A Natural Woman"

This groove is in 6/8 and used on many songs. Here is the basic groove:

Words and Music by Gerry Goffin, Carole King and Jerry Wexler
Copyright © 1967 Screen Gems-EMI Music Inc.
Copyright Renewed
All Rights Administered by Sony/ATV Music Publishing LLC, 424 Church Street, Suite 1200, Nashville, TN 37219
International Copyright Secured   All Rights Reserved

Additional Listening

"Take Five" Dave Brubeck (5/4)

"Theme from Mission: Impossible" Lalo Schifrin (5/4)

"Money" Pink Floyd (7/4)

"Nothing Else Matters" Metallica (6/8)

"Turn It on Again" Genesis (6/4 and 7/4)

"Manic Depression" The Jimi Hendrix Experience (3/4)

"Seven Days" Sting (5/8)

TRIPLETS

In order to understand how to play the next groove, we need to discuss triplets. A *triplet* is a rhythm comprised of three evenly divided eighth notes in the space of one quarter note. They are beamed together with the number "3" placed above or below the beam. The eighth-note triplets below show the two popular ways they are counted.

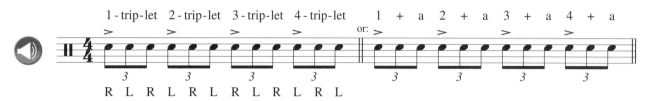

The next step is to practice going back and forth between straight eighth notes, 16th notes, and eighth-note triplets. Perform this exercise while sitting at your drum kit, playing quarter notes on the hi-hat pedal with your left foot:

Now that you can hear what they sound like, we're going to place a tie underneath the first two triplets. So, we are playing just the first and third triplets but still counting the second triplet, which is not played because it is joined together with the first triplet. This is called a *shuffle feel* or a *swing feel*.

Below is another way of notating it. Adding an eighth rest in place of the second triplet eliminates the need for a tie.

NOTATING A SHUFFLE FEEL

Writing an entire piece of music using the triplet notation can be tedious and look confusing. Instead of doing this, we simply write eighth notes as we normally would but include an indicator at the top of the sheet music to tell the musician that the eighth notes are to be *swung*, or played with a shuffle feel.

Shuffle feel

There also may be a notated indicator at the top of the sheet music that simply means the regular eighth notes are to be swung:

THE SHUFFLE

The shuffle is a very popular groove. It's used in a variety of music styles and there are different types of shuffles to play.

The Texas Shuffle

The Texas shuffle is used a lot in blues music. This style can be performed with the right hand playing quarter notes or swung eighth notes. The left hand is **very** important in this groove. It plays swung eighth notes on the snare, with accents played on beats 2 and 4. Parentheses are included around notes that are to be *ghosted*, or played softly. The bass drum plays quarter notes. The same beat is notated in two different ways here:

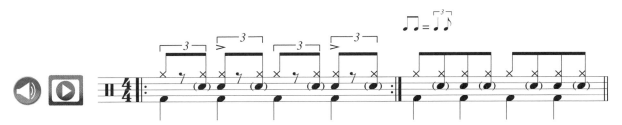

The Rock Shuffle

The rock shuffle is used in a variety of musical styles. Below are some examples of this type of shuffle at different tempos. The ghosted snare drum—again, notated with parentheses—is also important in this groove.

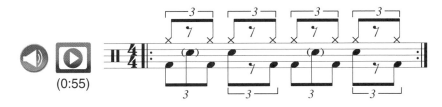

(0:55)

> **Additional Listening**
>
> "Pride and Joy" Stevie Ray Vaughan and Double Trouble
> "Sweet Home Chicago" Robert Johnson
> "Roadhouse Blues" The Doors
>
> "Lido Shuffle" Boz Scaggs
> "Hot for Teacher" Van Halen

THE HALF-TIME SHUFFLE

Here is a basic half-time shuffle with the snare drum on beat 3.

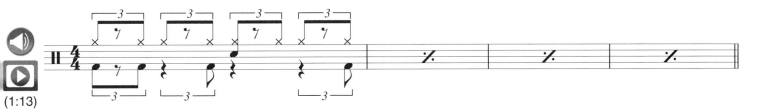

(1:13)

"Babylon Sisters"

This Steely Dan classic is a great take on the half-time shuffle.

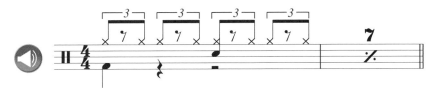

Words and Music by Walter Becker and Donald Fagen
Copyright © 1980 Zeon Music (ASCAP) and Freejunket Music (ASCAP)
International Copyright Secured   All Rights Reserved

> **Additional Listening:**
>
> "Fool in the Rain" Led Zeppelin
> "Rosanna" Toto

LESSON 13

THE 12/8 GROOVE

The 12/8 groove has a very distinct feel. This groove can be identified almost immediately and can vary from being relatively easy to extremely challenging. It is used quite a bit in blues music and is also heard a lot in popular music.

The time signature's top number tells you that there are 12 beats in a measure, with the eighth note receiving one full beat/count. It will be a little easier to count the eighth notes like triplets: either "1-trip-let, 2-trip-let, 3-trip-let, 4-trip-let" or "1-and-uh, 2-and-uh, 3-and-uh, 4-and-uh" instead of "1-2-3, 4-5-6, 7-8-9, 10-11-12."

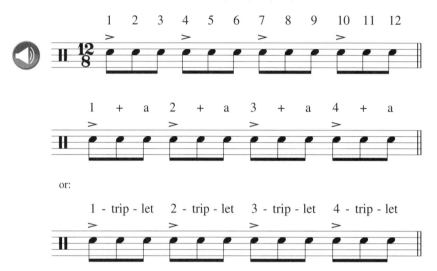

Examples in 12/8 could also be written in 6/8 by cutting the measures in half and playing them as two bars of six eighth notes.

Below are typical grooves in 12/8, with the bass drum playing on beats 1 and 3 (or beats 1 and 7 if counting to 12) and the snare playing on beats 2 and 4 (or beats 4 and 10 if counting in 12). The dotted quarter note now equals three beats (i.e., three eighth notes).

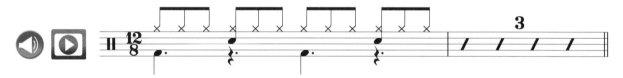

Here are a few more examples in 12/8, with different bass drum variations.

Additional Listening

"Red House" The Jimi Hendrix Experience

"The Sky Is Crying" Stevie Ray Vaughan and Double Trouble

"Lovin', Touchin', Squeezin'" Journey

"Rocky Mountain Way" Joe Walsh

OTHER POPULAR 12/8 GROOVES

"Hold the Line"

Here is an example of a pop song with a 12/8 groove:

Words and Music by David Paich
Copyright © 1978 Hudmar Publishing Co., Inc.
All Rights Controlled and Administered by Spirit Two Music, Inc.
International Copyright Secured   All Rights Reserved

"Everybody Wants to Rule the World"

This one involves playing hi-hat accents on every other eighth note, so it may take some extra practice. It's a very practical drum groove to know and play well.

Words and Music by Ian Stanley, Roland Orzabal and Christopher Hughes
Copyright © 1985 BMG VM Music Ltd. and BMG 10 Music Limited
All Rights Administered by BMG Rights Management (US) LLC
All Rights Reserved   Used by Permission

"Whipping Post"

There is an introduction in 11/8, but here is the 12/8 groove when the song kicks in. Also note that there are two drummers playing on the original recording, so this example is an arrangement for one drummer:

Words and Music by Gregg Allman
© 1970, 1971 (Renewed) UNICHAPPELL MUSIC, INC. and ELIJAH BLUE MUSIC
All Rights Reserved   Used by Permission

"Minute by Minute"

This is another tricky but great groove to play. Pay close attention to the bass drum pattern.

Words and Music by Michael McDonald and Lester Abrams
Copyright © 1978 Snug Music and BMG Firefly
All Rights for Snug Music Administered by Wixen Music Publishing, Inc.
All Rights for BMG Firefly Administered by BMG Rights Management (US) LLC
All Rights Reserved   Used by Permission

LESSON 14

TRIPLET FILLS

This lesson will help you get used to playing triplet fills, as opposed to the straight fills you learned in Lessons 4 and 5. For the following examples, play a shuffle groove for the first three measures, then a triplet fill for the fourth measure. Notice above each example are several different ways you might see the shuffle feel indicated in drum music.

QUARTER-NOTE TRIPLETS

The example below abbreviates "one-trip-let" as "1-T-L" to show how the counting lines up between eighth-note triplets (top) and quarter-note triplets (bottom). You can see that the quarter-note triplets line up with every other eighth-note triplet.

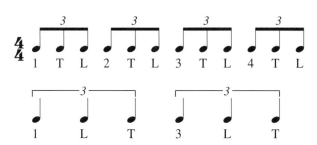

The following exercise can help you smoothly transition from eighth-note triplets to quarter-note triplets. Play the hi-hat pedal in quarter notes (not shown).

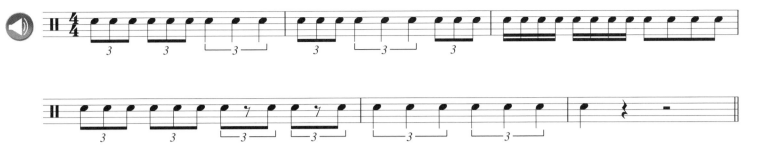

16TH-NOTE TRIPLETS

Sixteenth-note triplets have a double beam connecting the note stems and have exactly double the number of notes (six) as eighth-note triplets (three) per beat. You count 16th-note triplets as "1-trip-let-And-trip-let, 2-trip-let-And-trip-let, 3-trip-let-And-trip-let, 4-trip-let-And-trip-let" (noted below as "1-T-L-+-T-L, 2-T-L-+-T-L, 3-T-L-+-T-L, 4-T-L-+-T-L").

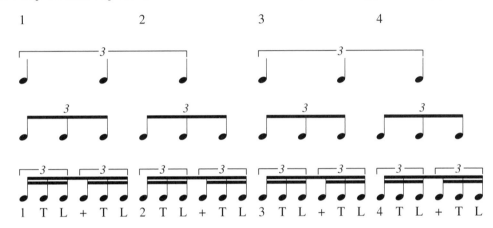

Since 16th-note triplets are generally fast by nature, counting that many notes while trying to play them can be difficult. While it's important to understand how to count them, it's recommended that you know how they feel when played rather than counting them. This takes time, but it will eventually happen if you practice them. This drum kit solo will be helpful in this regard:

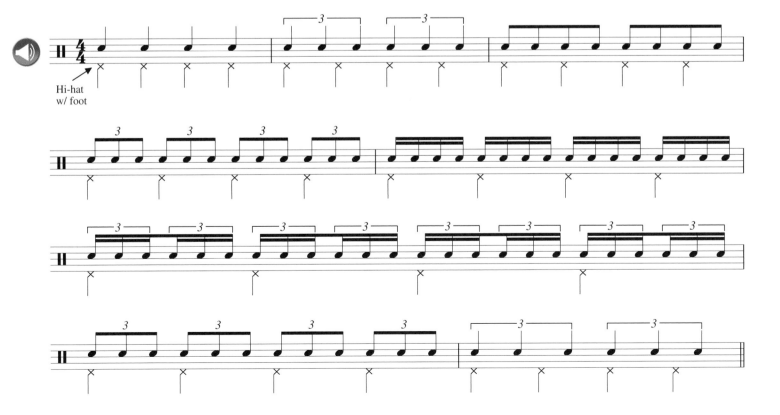

LESSON 15

Demo   Play-Along

"LA GRANGE"

Intro
Moderately fast ♩ = 163

Verse

Guitar Solo

Words and Music by Billy F Gibbons, Dusty Hill and Frank Lee Beard
Copyright © 1973 Music Of Stage Three
Copyright Renewed
All Rights Administered by Stage Three Music (US) Inc., a BMG Chrysalis company
All Rights Reserved   Used by Permission

Play 14 times

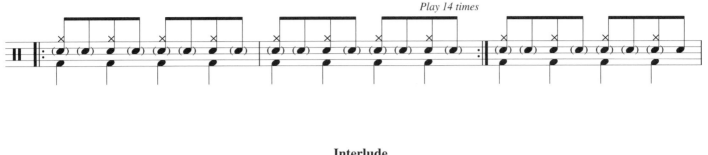

Interlude

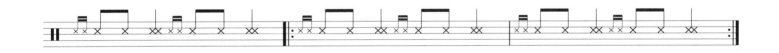

Outro-Guitar Solo

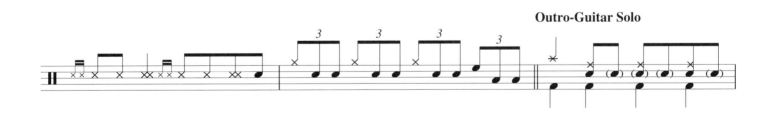

Repeat and fade

ABOUT THE AUTHOR

Alan Arber is an award-winning drummer and teacher in the greater Milwaukee and Chicago areas. Alan plays all genres of music, ranging from trios to drumming for full symphonies. He has performed at countless festivals, clubs, and theaters.

Alan endorses Paiste cymbals and is the drummer for Daryl Stuermer (Jean Luc Ponty, Genesis, Phil Collins guitarist) and the Altered Five Blues Band, and has toured all over the world.

Audio Credits

Alan Arber: Drums

Raymond Tevich: Keyboards

Jay Craggs: Guitar/Engineer

John Wheeler: Bass

Recorded, Engineered, and Mixed at Stoic Media